Joshua

PURSUING THE PROMISES OF GOD

LEADER MATERIALS

Joshua: Pursuing the Promises of God, Leader Materials

ISBN: 9798374884746

ACKNOWLEDGMENTS

Directors of Seek and Find
Project Managers, Lead Writers and Editors
Christi Davis and Summer Lacy

Layout/design
Gillian Unruh

Edits and Review
Jean Muñoz

LEADER MATERIALS
Table of Contents

HOW TO USE THESE MATERIALS

Welcome! We are thankful that you are studying Joshua: Pursuing the Promises of God, and we are excited that you are leading a small group through the study of this amazing book of the Bible. We strongly believe in the power of discipleship and in the importance of growing our understanding of God's word in community. We have seen first hand the tremendous impact that small group discussion can have on the life of a Bible study and on the good of those who participate in it.

The small group leader plays a significant role in the health and productivity of the group, so we have created the following resources to contribute to the training of those leaders and to assist them in the facilitation of their small group discussions each week.

First, you will find a Leader Training Guide. This guide provides general leader training material. It is designed to give an in-depth understanding of our Bible study process, an overview of the role of a small group leader and to provide tips for leading a small group well.

Second, you will find a Small Group Discussion Guide. This resource consists of a breakdown of each week of study, including a subset of questions from the study guide that we believe will produce a fruitful discussion of each week's material.

Thank you for studying with Seek and Find! We hope these materials are helpful. You can find additional studies, resources and downloads at www.SeekandFindStudies.com

Joshua
PURSUING THE PROMISES OF GOD

LEADER TRAINING GUIDE

THE GOAL: GROWTH

Our foundational goal is that each person involved, from students to leaders to teachers, would experience spiritual growth through their participation in Bible study. We define growth as follows:

Growth in their individual relationships with God, including their:

    a. <u>Knowledge of God</u>
       Growing in their understanding of who God is, what He does, and what He is like;

    b. <u>Faith in God</u>
       Growing in their belief that God is who He says He is and will do what He says He will do;

    c. <u>Trust in God</u>
       Growing in consistently inviting God into the details of their lives, believing He will do more than they can ask, think, or imagine;

    d. <u>Ability to discern God's leading</u>
       Growing in their ability to notice the work of the Spirit in their lives and discern where He is leading them; and

    e. <u>Obedience to God</u>
       Growing in both the quality and immediacy of their obedience. When they know what God desires they do, they put it into practice more quickly and more precisely.

Growth in their relationships with one another:

    a. Coming to know other members of the body of Christ more deeply;

    b. Building authentic connections with other believers;

    c. Encouraging each other in their faith; and

    d. Serving each other in practical ways.

Always allow the goal of growth to guide your interactions with small group members. How can you encourage the growth of those you interact with or experience growth yourself?

THE PROCESS: HANDS ON LEARNING

One of the primary goals of our curriculum is to facilitate hands-on learning. This type of learning is active; it encourages students to discover truth for themselves. In order for this to happen, students must be experientially engaged in the learning process.

To this end, each week of study is divided into three distinct parts: <u>Listen</u>, <u>Lean In</u>, and <u>Learn</u>.

Students begin by studying the Word themselves. As they do, they learn to <u>Listen</u> to what God says through His Word.

    a. First, they read for comprehension, asking what does the text say?

    b. Next, they attempt to interpret the text, asking what does the text mean?

    c. Finally, they turn to application, considering what God is drawing their attention to and how He desires they respond.

Students then <u>Lean In</u> to community by discussing the passage with others. This allows them the opportunity to process what they've learned and hear the thoughts, insights and opinions of others. Students are able to both encourage others and be encouraged by their small group members.

Finally, students, <u>Learn</u> as they listen to a teaching designed to address potential areas of confusion and challenge participants to discern the Lord's leading and respond in faith.

The order of our process is important. Allowing learners space to actively and independently interact with Scripture is essential to their growth. This means that hands-on learning will often be messy. It will take time for students to learn how to navigate this type of study. Help to focus participants' attention on perseverance rather than perfection.

THE IMPORTANCE OF SMALL GROUPS

Every component of our Bible study process is important. Solid curriculum and insightful teachings are hallmarks of a good study. However, it is the Small Group discussion time that draws participants back semester after semester.

We have found the following to be true regarding our Small Groups:

Individual insights are solidified and deepened
Explaining to others the insights they have had during individual time of study provides an opportunity for each student to deepen their personal understanding of the material.

New revelation often occurs
Hearing other students' perceptions provides an opportunity to consider things they might not have noticed in the text.

Ideas are tested
Whether hearing responses to their own answers or responding to the answers of others, students learn to test ideas honestly and compassionately.

Discipleship takes place
Small Groups provide an opportunity for discipleship, without much effort on the part of anyone; believers naturally glean understanding and insight from other believers.

Relationships are fostered
Relationships develop and mature more quickly when Small Group members are open and vulnerable. Many opportunities present themselves for members to support and care for each other.

Confidence is built
Over time, students become more comfortable and confident with the process of studying and discussing Scripture, which builds their confidence to do so.

In order to lead effectively, you must first understand the role of a Small Group Leader – what it is and what it is not.

What it IS

As a Small Group Leader, you are a <u>fellow student</u>.
Do not answer every question directed to you as the group leader; instead, turn questions into opportunities for discussion. Pose questions asked of you to the entire group instead of feeling the need to answer the question yourself.

As a Small Group Leader, you are a <u>conversation facilitator</u>.
Your goal is to facilitate a productive group conversation, where everyone has the opportunity to contribute some and no member dominates too much. Some weeks you may need to share more, in order to keep the discussion going. Other weeks you may find that you share less, or not at all. Model transparency and authenticity early and often in order to encourage others to do the same.

As a Small Group Leader, you are a <u>community-builder</u>.
Look for ways to build group community. The more you can involve others, the better!

As a Small Group Leader, you are a <u>disciple-maker</u>.
Aim to encourage each individual member to grow deeper in their faith.

What it is NOT

The Small Group Leader role is not one of <u>teacher</u>.
Although you may be gifted to teach, this is not the role you are to fill as a Small Group Leader. By doing so, you are enabling students to short circuit the learning process. Instead of working to discover truth for themselves, they will come to depend on you to reveal it to them.

The Small Group Leader role is not <u>personality-driven</u>.
There are many types of personalities that make excellent small group leaders. You do not need to be naturally out-going or charismatic. You just need to have the time and the heart to pray for and serve your group.

LEADING A GROUP EFFECTIVELY

There are several different ways you can set the stage for a positive and productive small group environment.

Establish prayer as a priority. Although our small group time will be focused on the study of God's word, be sure to pray often, outside of small group, for the discussion and the members of your group.

Prepare in advance
   a. Pray for each member of your group and over the time you have together.

   b. Complete your homework each week.

   c. Try to predict any issues or concerns (especially sensitive topics) group members may have within the assigned portion of Scripture.

   d. Review the Small Group Discussion Guide and determine which questions you want to discuss. Be sure to plan on the amount of time you want to spend in each section and allot your group time accordingly.

Communicate consistently with your group
   a. If possible, email your group before the first meeting. Introduce yourself, provide meeting time, place and include any necessary logistical information.

   b. At least once a week, send a communication to your small group with links to teachings and other thoughts / encouragement.

   c. Try to have a one-on-one conversation with each group member over the course of the semester.

   d. Follow-up on questions, issues, concerns or prayer requests brought up in the small group.

Build community among group members
   a. Facilitate connections among the members of your group.

   b. If possible, organize a time outside of Bible study to gather with your small group members at least once a semester. You can even assign this task to one of your group members!

Make discipleship a priority
   a. Direct participants to outside resources as necessary.

   b. Intentionally look for and raise up other leaders.

The first meeting sets the stage for every other meeting that follows. Review the following expectations with group members on day one.

Come Prepared. Come with homework done and ready to discuss. Some of you might be able to complete all the questions, while some may only get through the Comprehend section. Either way is fine, but come prepared to discuss what you have learned.

Talk and Listen. We won't have enough time to hear from every person on every question. For those of you who like to talk, focus on creating space and silence for others to share. For those who tend to be quieter, make an effort to let us hear from you!

Stay on Topic. Let's work to stay focused on what we have gathered to do: Study the Bible.

    a. Avoid Cross-talk: Cross-talk occurs when one person answers a question and someone else shares their experience in that area or gives advice regarding that person's situation. Cross-talk tends to take the group off topic. Instead, follow-up after class.

    b. Avoid topics revolving around denominational or political preferences.

    c. Avoid sharing things you have heard from pastors or teachers, or read in books. Although it can be helpful, this takes away from the time we have to discuss the passage itself and what you personally have learned from studying it.

Be Mindful of Time. We will start and end on time, every time, as a way of honoring the commitment each of you have made to be here. If you come in late, or have to leave early, we understand! Please do so in a way that doesn't interrupt the discussion.

Practice Humility. Although you may not agree with everything that is shared in small group, remain open to hearing from others. Consider new perspectives and always remain respectful.

Avoid "We/You" statements. Instead use "I" statements, which help us avoid generalizations and lead to much more personalized answers.

Be Encouraging. Each person is at a different place in their spiritual walk. When expressing opinions, do so without a critical tone. Focus on encouraging and building each other up!

Be Transparent. Do your best to be real about who you are and what your life really looks like. You should feel free to express doubts and struggles.

Keep Confidence. This group is confidential. Be careful not to repeat anything outside of the group.

Use Caution when sharing about others. Proceed carefully when sharing about your spouse, friends and family. Honor others with your speech as you talk about them within small group.

Invest Yourself. Make an investment in the people in this group. Pray with and for each other. Show genuine care and concern for one another. Be quick to forgive one another if you are offended.

ESTABLISHING A WEEKLY FOCUS

As one week of study progresses to the next, the needs of your group will change. Group members will grow individually and the dynamics of group interaction will shift. As these things occur, you can help focus your group on progressing well through the study.

Consider the following points of focus for each week of study.

Week 1
Set the stage by discussing the process. Be open about how important it is for everyone to invest in the group through participation. Consider asking who is comfortable being called on randomly and who is not. Assure those that don't want to be called on randomly, that they will not be! Members who are talkative can choose a couple of questions they really want to answer and those that don't like to contribute can pick a couple they would be comfortable answering.

Weeks 1-3
Focus on building relationships and getting the group comfortable sharing. Encourage group members to choose 2-5 questions they would like to share on. Look for opportunities to model and encourage openness and vulnerability. Perhaps you or someone you know in the group can share something to set the stage?

Weeks 4-6
Encourage perseverance as life gets busy. Continue to encourage group members to do as much as they can and to continue to come! Consider meeting outside of group for a social event.

Weeks 7-8
Encourage finishing strong…or just showing up!

Week 9
Encourage reflection on what they've learned. Reviewing and reflecting is an important part of incorporating changes into our lives. Encourage your group to do the study reflection and use the time between studies to dig further into areas that have stood out to them.

NAVIGATING COMMON ISSUES

Every small group will have its issues. This is to be expected and is okay! As a leader, you should be prepared for issues to arise. Here are some common group discussion issues and ways you can handle them. First and foremost, always make sure to include prayer as a part of your preparation process.

1. The entire group is quiet:

  a. Leave longer pauses after asking questions. This could cause those on the fence about answering to have the courage to do so.

  b. Try sharing your answer first and then inviting other perspectives. (i.e. "Did anyone think about this differently?")

  c. Try providing the whole group the questions you are planning to discuss ahead of time and ask them to share for one or two.

  d. Ask someone you know to share something ahead of time.

2. The whole group is difficult to keep on topic:

  a. Be consistent in reminding the group of the purpose of our meetings – to study and discuss the Bible!

  b. Redirect back to the text as much as needed.

3. The group has some people that know each other well and others that are new:

  a. Outside of group, ask those that know each other well to help in making new group members feel included. Ask them to sit apart or sit by a new member.

  b. Keep the discussion focused on the content of the study.

  c. Make sure everyone who wants to share gets the chance to do so.

  d. Have meals or coffee as a group outside of group time, allowing group members the chance to get to know each other.

4. One person in the group is quiet:

  a. Try sitting across from that person and making eye contact. This can signal that you'd like to hear from them.

  b. Check in with that person outside of group time to figure out if there's some issue, or if this is just their personality.

  c. Make sure they know that you would value their perspective, but you will not put them on the spot.

  d. Give them the questions you plan to discuss in group ahead of time and ask if there are any they'd be willing to answer.

5. Someone is consistently sarcastic and it affects the group:

  a. Try to find a way to have them answer a question where their answer would need to be open or vulnerable.

  b. Have a discussion with them outside of the group.

6. One person dominates group discussion time:

    a. Avoid making eye contact, which can be perceived as you wanting them to answer.

    b. Try sitting next to them. You will not be so likely to make eye contact and can interrupt gently, if needed, to keep the conversation moving. Maybe say something like, "I wish we could spend longer on this question, but I'm guessing we are going to need some extra time for a couple of the other questions…how about we come back to this if we have time?"

    c. Create opportunities outside of small group to have discussions. Walk out to the parking lot together after study, invite them for coffee. Some group members may require more attention than others.

    d. After the person who is dominating shares, ask if anyone else had different thoughts, or wants to speak to the same point.

7. Someone gives a wrong answer:

    a. Thank them for sharing.

    b. Say you thought of it differently, and share your answer peacefully. Do not disagree aggressively or sarcastically.

    c. Offer to research the question further, or ask one of the teachers/leaders of the study for insight or clarification.

    d. Remember, it is not your job to teach, only to facilitate the discussion, but you can offer evidence or reasons for your answer.

8. Someone shares something troubling:

    a. First, take time to check your understanding of what was shared. Make sure you didn't interpret something the wrong way.

    b. Second, is everyone safe? Do they need outside help or counseling? Take them aside after the discussion and let them know these things are available to them.

    c. Follow up. Follow up. Follow up.

9. Someone says something that offends someone else:

    a. Remember that your job is to be sensitive to everyone in the group.

    b. Try to be a peacemaker, smoothing things over as best you can. Sometimes you may need to summarize or address the concerns of both sides or just empathize with both sides. Sometimes it is best to just move on and talk to both parties separately after class. The goal is that everyone feels like they can be transparent and vulnerable, without being judged.

We began this training guide by laying before you our goal for those of us involved in this study – growth. One of the things we must remember is that growth is always accompanied by periods of discomfort. As we grow in our knowledge of and love for the Lord, in fellowship with other believers, and in a deeper understanding of who we are and what purpose we serve, we'll be stretched! It will be uncomfortable, yet beneficial.

However, the beauty of the end is well worth the discomfort of the means.

Keep your mind trained on progress and perseverance instead of perfection. Keep the end goal of growth in mind and aim for productive discussions, understanding of course that <u>productive</u> does not always equal <u>pleasant</u>!

A productive group discussion has the following components:

1. Everyone learns.
2. All members of the group participate in (but none dominate) the discussion.
3. Participants can be open, honest, and vulnerable with their doubts, struggles, and fears.

Remember though, these types of discussions progress over time. Don't worry too much about each small group meeting; rather, look for improvement each week over the course of the nine weeks of study you have together.

Allow this process to help you depend on the Lord and wait patiently for Him – for your own growth, and for the growth of your small group members as well.

For more resources visit www.SeekandFindStudies.com/resources.

Joshua

PURSUING THE PROMISES OF GOD

SMALL GROUP DISCUSSION GUIDE

TIPS FOR USING THIS SMALL GROUP DISCUSSION GUIDE

We are excited to have you join our study Joshua: Pursuing the Promises of God. This guide is intended to help you think through and navigate your small group discussions. It assumes approximately 45 minutes of focused discussion time each week, but can easily be altered to meet your group's specific needs. While 45 minutes is not enough time to discuss every Comprehend, Interpret and Apply question from the study guide, it does allow time to cover several questions from each section, reinforcing habits of effective Bible study. As a part of this guide, we have selected questions we think will contribute to a fruitful discussion of the major topics and themes from each week of study. However, we recommend that you review the suggested discussion questions and make modifications to address the needs of your group. That said, we do have some general suggestions for your small group time:

1. PLAN YOUR TIME
Time management can easily become the most challenging part of leading a small group. You can effectively manage your group time by planning which questions you definitely want to make time for, which additional questions you would like to cover if time allows, and which questions you can skip if you are short on time. Many leaders find it helpful to put times next to specific questions or sections so they can gauge if they are running ahead or behind and adjust accordingly.

2. WORK METHODICALLY THROUGH THE SECTIONS
It may be tempting to jump right to the Interpret questions in your group discussion, but we caution against that. The Comprehend questions lay a good foundation for looking first at what the word of God says, which is an important step that is sometimes skipped in Bible study. Additionally, these questions are generally more straight-forward; they provide participants with a way to ease into deeper, more challenging questions. And finally, some participants may have only completed the Comprehend section. Skipping this part of group discussion could result in leaving people out of the discussion altogether. Over time, we think you will find that Comprehend is a critical part of your group discussions and provides the opportunity for you to successfully incorporate all group members into the conversation.

3. PREPARE MOST FOR INTERPRET
Many of our groups have indicated that Interpret is where they spend the bulk of their time. As you get started, it likely makes sense to spend more time preparing for that section of discussion.

4. ADVICE REGARDING APPLY
The Apply section could be the easiest or hardest part of group discussion, depending on the openness of your group. For the first few sessions, we recommend you plan ways to model openness and authenticity. Perhaps, you can share something vulnerable, or ask someone in your group (ahead of time) to consider sharing something. You may also want to start by having larger groups break into groups of 2-3 to share before coming back together to wrap-up.

TIPS FOR USING THIS SMALL GROUP DISCUSSION GUIDE

5. REMEMBER THE GOAL

Above all, remember that the goal of this time is a productive group discussion, where honesty, authenticity, and vulnerability can grow over time. It is common for the first week or two to be very different from future weeks, as your group gets more comfortable with the study and discussion process.

More tips and tools for leading small groups are available at www.SeekandFindStudies.com.

6. KEEP THE ORDER OF THE PROCESS!

This study has been designed to help students grow in their ability to read and study the word of God. This requires that the student studies the text independently *before* engaging in a small group discussion of the text or listening to a teaching of the material. If the students in your group are not used to the order of this process, it will feel difficult at first. That's okay! Given time to adjust, your small group discussions will be far more rich when they occur *after* the students have studied on their own and *before* they hear from a teacher!

Below is a breakdown of the order of our study process for each week of study:

Week 1:

Since Week 1 is an introductory week, we follow a slightly different process.

- Begin by having the students watch or listen to the *Method of our Studies* video found at https://www.seekandfindstudies.com/our-curriculum.

- Next, go to Week 1 of the Small Group Discussion Guide and lead your group through pages 22-23.

- Last, students will watch the Introduction to Joshua teaching found at https://www.seekandfindstudies.com/joshua or, have a teacher from your group cover this material!

Weeks 2-9:

- First, students will "Listen" to God's voice through their individual time of study in the days prior to each week's Bible study meeting.

- Next, students will then "Lean In" to community through a small group discussion of the text.

- Finally, students will continue to "Learn" through a large group teaching on the material.

Strong and Courageous

GATHER / PREPARE – Greet participants as they arrive. Ensure that your roster is up-to-date.

PRAY (~5 minutes) – Open in prayer.

PERSONAL INTRODUCTIONS (~5 minutes) – Let's begin by introducing ourselves. Tell us about yourself! You can use Week 1's Lean In section on page 12 of your study guide to take notes or keep track of names.

STUDY INTRODUCTION (~20 minutes) – If participants have not watched the *Method of our Studies* video prior to your first group meeting, watch it together now at https://www.seekandfindstudies.com/our-curriculum.

After viewing, ask your group if they have any questions about how the study works.

SMALL GROUP GUIDELINES (~5 minutes) – Review the Small Group Discussion Guidelines on page 21 with your group. You may find it helpful to print these out and give a copy to each participant. After reviewing the guidelines, ask your group if they have any questions.

GROUP DISCUSSION (~10 minutes) – Go around the group and have each person answer the following questions:

- Why did you decide to come to this Bible study?

- What do you hope to gain from this study? From this small group time?

- What's one way our group can be praying for YOU over the next 9 weeks? (Just you, not your family, your neighbors, or anyone else. This is a safe place to share.)

WRAP-UP (~5 minutes)

1. Share with group members all the information on the "Important Links" page at the end of this resource.

2. Tell group members: By the next time we meet, you should work your way through the Week 2 Listen questions beginning on page 15 of your study guide. Do what you can and don't be discouraged if you can't make it through the entire week of questions. Remember that next week, you will come directly to small group when you arrive for Bible study.

3. Close in prayer

4. Dismiss to Large Group Teaching time. Teachings are available at www.SeekAndFindStudies.com/Joshua.

SMALL GROUP DISCUSSION GUIDELINES

Come Prepared. Come with homework done and ready to discuss. Some of you might be able to complete all the questions, while some may only get through the Comprehend section. Either way is fine, but come prepared to discuss what you have learned.

Talk and Listen. We won't have enough time to hear from every person on every question. For those of you who like to talk, focus on creating space and silence for others to share. For those who tend to be quieter, make an effort to let us hear from you!

Stay on Topic. Let's work to stay focused on what we have gathered to do: Study the Bible.
  a. Avoid Cross-talk: Cross-talk occurs when one person answers a question and someone else shares their experience in that area or gives advice regarding that person's situation. Cross-talk tends to take the group off topic. Instead, follow-up after class.
  b. Avoid topics revolving around denominational or political preferences.
  c. Avoid sharing things you have heard from pastors or teachers, or read in books. Although it can be helpful, this takes away from the time we have to discuss the passage itself and what you personally have learned from studying it.

Be Mindful of Time. We will start and end on time, every time, as a way of honoring the commitment each of you have made to be here. If you come in late, or have to leave early, we understand! Please do so in a way that doesn't interrupt the discussion.

Practice Humility. Although you may not agree with everything that is shared in small group, remain open to hearing from others. Consider new perspectives and always remain respectful.

Avoid "We/You" statements. Instead use "I" statements, which help us avoid generalizations and lead to much more personalized answers.

Be Encouraging. Each person is at a different place in their spiritual walk. When expressing opinions, do so without a critical tone. Focus on encouraging and building each other up!

Be Transparent. Do your best to be real about who you are and what your life really looks like. You should feel free to express doubts and struggles.

Keep Confidence. This group is confidential. Be careful not to repeat anything outside of the group.

Use Caution When Sharing About Others. Proceed carefully when sharing about your spouse, friends and family. Honor others with your speech as you talk about them within small group.

Invest Yourself. Make an investment in the people in this group. Pray with and for each other. Show genuine care and concern for one another. Be quick to forgive one another if you are offended.

Preparing to Receive the Promise

GATHER / PREPARE – As participants arrive, greet them and ask them to take a few minutes to skim over their answers to the homework questions, marking anything they would like the group to discuss.

PRAY / REFLECT (~5 minutes) – Open in prayer. Provide a brief summary of what we studied last week, and ask the following:

1. From the Reflect section, what from the introductory session made the most significant impact on you?

2. Was there anything from the teaching that stood out to you?

GROUP DISCUSSION – Remember, you will not be able to discuss every question or address every issue. Your goal is to have a productive discussion that covers the topics most needed by those in your group.

Comprehend (~5 minutes) – Use this time to ensure the group has a good grasp of what the text says. You may choose any questions from the Comprehend section, or use the ones listed below:

- **Page 19, #2** The Lord gave the people specific instructions, preparing them for what was to come. **(a)** What did He tell the people to do? (1:2) **(b)** What did He say He had already done? (1:3)

- **Page 19, #3** From Joshua 1:5: **(a)** What did the Lord promise He would do? **(b)** What did the Lord promise He would not do?

- **Page 19, #4** The Lord gave Joshua a series of instructions in Joshua 1:6-9. List everything the Lord commanded Joshua *to do/not* to do.

- **Page 20, #13** Summarize the primary focus of this section of Scripture in a single sentence.

- Were there any other questions from the Comprehend section that you would like to discuss? Were there any that you weren't sure how to answer, that you were confused about, or that made an impact on you?

Interpret (~20 minutes) – Use this time to discuss what the Biblical text means. You may choose any of the questions from the Interpret section, or use the ones below. Remind everyone that they are welcome to share their thoughts even if they were unable to complete the homework questions.

- **Page 21, #1 (a)** Briefly summarize the Lord's activity. **(b)** What characteristics of God did you notice?

- **Page 21, #2** The book of Joshua opens with the Lord commanding Joshua to prepare the people to cross over the Jordan. **(a)** What promise of God were the people preparing to receive? **(b)** This was not the Israelites' first attempt to receive this promise. What caused the previous generation to fail to receive God's promise?

- **Page 23, #5** Over the course of this study, we will learn much about godly leadership from Joshua. Turn to pg. 162. How had Joshua been prepared to take on the role of leading God's people into the Promised Land? How had Joshua demonstrated that he could be trusted for this very important role? How was Joshua assured that God wanted him to lead His people?

- **Page 24, #7** Throughout Scripture, God consistently uses stories and imagery to draw our attention to the Biblical theme of salvation. **(a)** Let's look at ways in which the salvation of Rahab points to the salvation God provided through Jesus Christ. From Romans 10:8-13, what must humanity declare of Jesus? How does the kindness of God spares us from death? What is the sure sign that Christ gives to believers? **(b)** Even the actions of the spies can bring to mind the actions of Jesus Christ. From Galatians 1:3-4, who gave His life for humanity? From Matthew 12 and Mark 10, how was the spies experience similar to Jesus'? **(c)** The instructions given to Rahab to avoid God's judgment are similar to the instructions God gave the Israelites at Passover to avoid judgment. What similarities did you see? **(d)** In considering the salvation imagery throughout Joshua Chapter 2, what had the greatest impact on you?

- **Page 25, #10** This week, the people of God prepared to receive the promises He had made to them. **(a)** What practical lessons can believers learn about preparation from Joshua and the Israelites? **(b)** Just as the Israelites prepared physically to receive God's promises, believers are to prepare spiritually. What do the following passages teach about that preparation? 1 Peter 1:13; 2 Timothy 2:21-26

- Were there any other questions from the Interpret section that you would like to discuss? Were there any that you weren't sure how to answer, that you were confused about, or that made an impact on you?

Apply (~10 minutes) – During this time, allow participants to talk through how the Lord has been speaking to them personally through this week's study. Have everyone turn to Page 26.

1. To what did the Lord draw your attention this week?

2. How can you respond?

WRAP-UP (~5 minutes)

1. Tell group members: By the next time we meet, you should work your way through the Week 3 Listen questions in your study guide. Do what you can and don't be discouraged if you can't make it through the entire week of questions!

2. Close in prayer

3. Dismiss to Large Group Teaching time. Teachings are available at www.SeekAndFindStudies.com/Joshua.

Crossing Over

GATHER / PREPARE – As participants arrive, greet them and ask them to take a few minutes to skim over their answers to the homework questions, marking anything they would like the group to discuss.

PRAY/ REFLECT (~5 minutes) – Open in prayer. Provide a brief summary of what we studied last week, and ask the following:

1. From the Reflect section, what made the most significant impact on you from the past week of study?

2. Was there anything from the teaching that stood out to you?

GROUP DISCUSSION – Remember, you will not be able to discuss every question or address every issue. Your goal is to have a productive discussion that covers the topics most needed by those in your group.

Comprehend (~5 minutes) – Use this time to ensure the group has a good grasp of what the text says. You may choose any questions from the Comprehend section, or use the ones listed below:

- **Page 35, #1** Early the next morning, Joshua and the Israelites set out for the Jordan River. What were they to follow when they crossed it? (3:3)

- **Page 35, #4** From Joshua 3:10, what two things would the Israelites know when the ark of the covenant went ahead of them into the Jordan?

- **Page 36, #11** God's miracle at the Jordan accomplished at least two things according to Joshua 4:24. **(a)** What would all the people of the earth know as a result of this miracle? **(b)** What would the result be for God's people?

- **Page 36, #17** Summarize the primary focus of this section of Scripture in a single sentence.

- Were there any other questions from the Comprehend section that you would like to discuss? Were there any that you weren't sure how to answer, that you were confused about, or that made an impact on you?

Interpret (~20 minutes) – Use this time to discuss what the Biblical text means. You may choose any of the questions from the Interpret section, or use the ones below. Remind everyone that they are welcome to share their thoughts even if they were unable to complete the homework questions.

- **Page 37, #1 (a)** Briefly summarize the Lord's activity. **(b)** What characteristics of God did you notice?

- **Page 37, #3** God wanted the people to know that He would be the one to dispossess the inhabitants of the land so that the Israelites could inherit it.

(a) From Psalm 24:1, what right does God have to take land from one people group and give it to another? **(b)** From the table, why was the Lord going to drive out these nations? Why was God giving the land to the Israelites? What did Moses warn them not to think regarding why God was giving them the land?

- **Page 39, #6** In Joshua Chapter 5, we encountered several topics of profound significance to Israel's relationship with God. **(a)** From the first table, circumcision was a sign of what? What did Passover commemorate and how was it related to circumcision? Why did they eat unleavened bread? What was the manna? **(b)** These topics still have profound significance to a believer's relationship with God. From the second table, what is true circumcision? Who is the true Passover lamb and what has He done? What does unleavened bread symbolize? Who is the true bread from heaven (manna) and what has He done? **(c)** What impacts you the most after closely considering these topics in both their Old and New Testaments contexts?

- **Page 41, #9** Joshua demonstrated godly leadership as the Israelites crossed into the Promised Land. Turn to pg. 163. What evidence did you see of Joshua's relationship with God in this week's passage? How was Joshua obedient to God? How did Joshua encourage the faith of the people?

- **Page 41, #10** This week, the people of God stepped out in faith and crossed over into the land the Lord was giving them. **(a)** What practical lessons can believers learn about faith from Joshua and the Israelites? **(b)** The Israelites stepped out in faith in order to receive God's promises, and believers must do the same. What did you learn about faith from Hebrews 11:6? Romans 1:17? 1 Corinthians 2:4-5?

- Were there any other questions from the Interpret section that you would like to discuss? Were there any that you weren't sure how to answer, that you were confused about, or that made an impact on you?

Apply (~10 minutes) – During this time, allow participants to talk through how the Lord has been speaking to them personally through this week's study. Have everyone turn to Page 42.

1. To what did the Lord draw your attention this week?

2. How can you respond?

WRAP-UP (~5 minutes)

1. Tell group members: Next week, we will discuss your answers to the Week 4 Listen questions from your study guide. I look forward to hearing your insights and questions!

2. Close in prayer

3. Dismiss to Large Group Teaching time. Teachings are available at www.SeekAndFindStudies.com/Joshua.

Faith or Judgment

GATHER / PREPARE - As participants arrive, greet them and ask them to take a few minutes to skim over their answers to the homework questions, marking anything they would like the group to discuss.

PRAY / REFLECT (~5 minutes) - Open in prayer. Provide a brief summary of what we studied last week, and ask the following:

1. From the Reflect section, what made the most significant impact on you from the past week of study?

2. Was there anything from the teaching that stood out to you?

GROUP DISCUSSION - Remember, you will not be able to discuss every question or address every issue. Your goal is to have a productive discussion that covers the topics most needed by those in your group.

Comprehend (~5 minutes) - Use this time to ensure the group has a good grasp of what the text says. You may choose any questions from the Comprehend section, or use the ones listed below:

- **Page 54, #1** When Joshua was near Jericho, he encountered a man "with a drawn sword in his hand." **(a)** What question did Joshua ask him? (5:13) **(b)** How did he respond? (5:14)

- **Page 54, #3** According to Joshua 6:2, what did the Lord say He had already done?

- **Page 54, #6** The Israelites were given a warning concerning the things set apart. What would happen if they disobeyed: To them, personally? To the camp of Israel as a whole? (6:18)

- **Page 55, #10** Next, Joshua commanded an unsuccessful attack against the city of Ai. **(a)** How many men were struck down? (7:5) **(b)** What impact did this have on the people? (7:5) **(c)** How did Joshua respond? (7:6-9)

- **Page 55, #15** How did Joshua and the Israelites respond to the Lord after their victory at Ai? List everything you see. (8:30-35)

- **Page 55, #16** Summarize the primary focus of this section of Scripture in a single sentence.

- Were there any other questions from the Comprehend section that you would like to discuss? Were there any that you weren't sure how to answer, that you were confused about, or that made an impact on you?

Interpret (~20 minutes) - Use this time to discuss what the Biblical text means. You may choose any of the questions from the Interpret section, or use the ones below. Remind everyone that they are welcome to share their thoughts even if they were unable to complete the homework questions.

- **Page 50, #1 (a)** Briefly summarize the Lord's activity. **(b)** What characteristics of God did you notice?

- **Page 57, #3** The Israelites' entrance to the Promised Land at Jericho was the fulfillment of one of God's great promises to them, and it was announced by trumpets and a loud shout. From 1 Thessalonians 4:16-17, what future promise of God will be announced in the same way?

- **Page 57, #4** The Israelites' entrance to the Promised Land was the fulfillment of one of God's great promises to them. This same event, however, meant judgment for the inhabitants of the land. **(a)** What did you learn about God's judgment from Psalm 9:8? Jeremiah 17:10? Ezekiel 18:30-32? John 3:16-21? **(b)** Just as the Israelites' entrance to the Promised Land meant judgment for the Canaanites, Christ's return will mean judgment for all who have not accepted salvation through Jesus Christ. How did you summarize the message from 2 Peter 3:1-13?

- **Page 59, #9** Joshua's faith was tested and proven through both the victories Israel won and the defeats they suffered. Turn to pg. 163. What evidence did you see of Joshua's relationship with God in this week's passage? How was Joshua obedient to God? How did Joshua encourage the faith of the people?

- **Page 59, #10** This week's passage highlights two extremes: faith, which leads to victory, and unbelief, which leads to judgment. **(a)** Hebrews 11:30-31 tells us that the Israelites marching around Jericho and Rahab's actions demonstrated faith. What other instances of faith do you see from this week's passage? **(b)** The opposite of faith is unbelief. From this week's passage, what did unbelief look like in the inhabitants of Canaan? In God's people? **(c)** What does James 2:14-26 teach about true faith?

- Were there any other questions from the Interpret section that you would like to discuss? Were there any that you weren't sure how to answer, that you were confused about, or that made an impact on you?

Apply (~10 minutes) – During this time, allow participants to talk through how the Lord has been speaking to them personally through this week's study. Have everyone turn to Page 60.

1. To what did the Lord draw your attention this week?

2. How can you respond?

WRAP-UP (~5 minutes)

1. Tell group members: At our next meeting, we will discuss your answers to the Week 5 Listen questions from your study guide. Make note of anything that you have questions about as you study and we'll make sure to discuss.

2. Close in prayer

3. Dismiss to Large Group Teaching time. Teachings are available at www.SeekAndFindStudies.com/Joshua.

Leaving Nothing Undone

GATHER / PREPARE - As participants arrive, greet them and ask them to take a few minutes to skim over their answers to the homework questions, marking anything they would like the group to discuss.

PRAY / REFLECT (~5 minutes) - Open in prayer. Provide a brief summary of what we studied last week, and ask the following:

1. From the Reflect section, what made the most significant impact on you from the past week of study?

2. Was there anything from the teaching that stood out to you?

GROUP DISCUSSION - Remember, you will not be able to discuss every question or address every issue. Your goal is to have a productive discussion that covers the topics most needed by those in your group.

Comprehend (~5 minutes) - Use this time to ensure the group has a good grasp of what the text says. You may choose any questions from the Comprehend section, or use the ones listed below:

- **Page 73, #1** What action did the kings west of the Jordan take after hearing about the events at Jericho and Ai? (9:2)

- **Page 73, #2** The Gibeonites took a different approach. Summarize their plan. (9:3-6)

- **Page 73, #3** What did the Israelites fail to do in Joshua 9:14?

- **Page 73, #7** From Joshua 10:9-14, What did you see for actions taken by Joshua / the Israelites? What did you see for actions taken by the Lord?

- **Page 74, #11** According to Joshua 10:42, why was Joshua able to capture all these kings and their land in one campaign?

- **Page 74, #18** Summarize the primary focus of this section of Scripture in a single sentence.

- Were there any other questions from the Comprehend section that you would like to discuss? Were there any that you weren't sure how to answer, that you were confused about, or that made an impact on you?

Interpret (~20 minutes) - Use this time to discuss what the Biblical text means. You may choose any of the questions from the Interpret section, or use the ones below. Remind everyone that they are welcome to share their thoughts even if they were unable to complete the homework questions.

- **Page 75, #1 (a)** Briefly summarize the Lord's activity. **(b)** What characteristics of God did you notice?

- **Page 75, #2** When the Gibeonites heard about the defeat of Jericho and Ai, they acted deceptively in order to secure peace with Israel and avoid the same fate. **(a)** What could the Israelites have done to avoid being bound to this oath? (Consider Joshua 2:17-20 and 9:14.) **(b)** What can we learn about God from the fact that He did not intervene in the situation or prevent the treaty?

- **Page 76, #5** Joshua 11:19 tells us that of all the inhabitants of Canaan, only the Gibeonites sought peace and were spared God's judgment. **(a)** From Romans 5:1, how can humanity obtain peace with God? **(b)** In order to obtain peace, the Gibeonites surrendered their cities and became Israel's servants. From Romans 6:16-23, how does this point to what humanity must do?

- **Page 77, #8** Joshua set an example for all believers as he left "nothing undone" of all God commanded. Turn to pg. 163. What evidence did you see of Joshua's relationship with God in this week's passage? How was Joshua obedient to God? How did Joshua encourage the faith of the people?

- **Page 77, #9** In this week's passage, the Israelites followed God's lead as they engaged in many battles for their inheritance. **(a)** What practical lessons can believers learn about following God's lead from Joshua and the Israelites? **(b)** The Israelites battled in pursuit of God's promises, as must believers. What did you see about what we fight against and how we are to fight from Galatians 5:24-25? 2 Corinthians 10:3-5? Titus 2:11-12? Ephesians 6:10-18?

- Were there any other questions from the Interpret section that you would like to discuss? Were there any that you weren't sure how to answer, that you were confused about, or that made an impact on you?

Apply (~10 minutes) – During this time, allow participants to talk through how the Lord has been speaking to them personally through this week's study. Have everyone turn to Page 78.

1. To what did the Lord draw your attention this week?

2. How can you respond?

WRAP-UP (~5 minutes)

1. Tell group members: We are more than halfway through the study! Next week, we'll be discussing the Week 6 Listen questions from your study guide. I encourage you to really persevere as we head into the last half of the study.

2. Close in prayer

3. Dismiss to Large Group Teaching time. Teachings are available at www.SeekAndFindStudies.com/Joshua.

An Unconquered Inheritance

GATHER / PREPARE – As participants arrive, greet them and ask them to take a few minutes to skim over their answers to the homework questions, marking anything they would like the group to discuss.

PRAY / REFLECT (~5 minutes) – Open in prayer. Provide a brief summary of what we studied last week, and ask the following:

1. From the Reflect section, what made the most significant impact on you from the past week of study?

2. Was there anything from the teaching that stood out to you?

GROUP DISCUSSION – Remember, you will not be able to discuss every question or address every issue. Your goal is to have a productive discussion that covers the topics most needed by those in your group.

Comprehend (~5 minutes) – Use this time to ensure the group has a good grasp of what the text says. You may choose any questions from the Comprehend section, or use the ones listed below:

- **Page 91, #1** What observation did the Lord make about the land in Joshua 13:1?

- **Page 91, #2** From Joshua 13:6: **(a)** What did God say He would do regarding the inhabitants of the land? **(b)** What was the "only" thing God commanded Joshua to do?

- **Page 92, #9** What did Caleb say the Lord had done for him? (14:10-11)

- **Page 92, #10** What did Caleb ask for and why? (14:12)

- **Page 92, #11** What does Joshua 15:14 tell us that Caleb was, in fact, able to do?

- **Page 93, #18** Summarize the primary focus of this section of Scripture in a single sentence.

- Were there any other questions from the Comprehend section that you would like to discuss? Were there any that you weren't sure how to answer, that you were confused about, or that made an impact on you?

Interpret (~20 minutes) – Use this time to discuss what the Biblical text means. You may choose any of the questions from the Interpret section, or use the ones below. Remind everyone that they are welcome to share their thoughts even if they were unable to complete the homework questions.

- **Page 94, #1 (a)** Briefly summarize the Lord's activity. **(b)** What characteristics of God did you notice?

- **Page 94, #2** As Chapter 13 opens, God told Joshua to distribute the land as an inheritance despite the fact that "a great deal of the land" remained unconquered. **(a)** Look at the Boundaries of the Twelve Tribes map on p. 165. What observations do you have about the work that remained? **(b)** How would distributing the unconquered lands motivate the people to persevere?

- **Page 94, #3** Joshua demonstrated godly leadership as he distributed the land as an inheritance. Turn to pg. 163. What evidence did you see of Joshua's relationship with God in this week's passage? How was Joshua obedient to God? How did Joshua encourage the faith of the people?

- **Page 96, #7** In Joshua Chapters 13-17, we saw several instances where the Israelites failed to drive out the inhabitants of the land. **(a)** What did God warn would happen if the Israelites failed to drive out the inhabitants of the land in Numbers 33:50-55? Exodus 23:33?

- **Page 97, #8** God had promised an inheritance to the Israelites. However, it was unconquered; they would have to act in order to receive it. This principle is seen throughout Scripture. **(a)** From the first table, what did God promise and what did the Israelites have to do from Exodus 12:21-23? Exodus 14:10-14? Exodus 16:4? Numbers 9:15-23? **(b)** Just as the Israelites had to act, so must we. From the second table, what does God promise and what must believers do from Matthew 11:28-30? John 15:4-5? James 1:12? 2 Peter 1:3-8?

- Were there any other questions from the Interpret section that you would like to discuss? Were there any that you weren't sure how to answer, that you were confused about, or that made an impact on you?

Apply (~10 minutes) – During this time, allow participants to talk through how the Lord has been speaking to them personally through this week's study. Have everyone turn to Page 98.

1. To what did the Lord draw your attention this week?

2. How can you respond?

WRAP-UP (~5 minutes)

1. Tell group members: Work your way through the Week 7 Listen questions from your study guide before our next meeting. I look forward to discussing it with you!

2. Close in prayer

3. Dismiss to Large Group Teaching time. Teachings are available at www.SeekAndFindStudies.com/Joshua.

Every Promise Fulfilled

GATHER / PREPARE – As participants arrive, greet them and ask them to take a few minutes to skim over their answers to the homework questions, marking anything they would like the group to discuss.

PRAY / REFLECT (~5 minutes) – Open in prayer. Provide a brief summary of what we studied last week, and ask the following:

1. From the Reflect section, what made the most significant impact on you from the past week of study?

2. Was there anything from the teaching that stood out to you?

GROUP DISCUSSION – Remember, you will not be able to discuss every question or address every issue. Your goal is to have a productive discussion that covers the topics most needed by those in your group.

Comprehend (~5 minutes) – Use this time to ensure the group has a good grasp of what the text says. You may choose any questions from the Comprehend section, or use the ones listed below:

- **Page 111, #1** Joshua Chapter 18 begins with the entire Israelite community assembled at Shiloh. What did they set up there? (18:1)

- **Page 111, #3** Joshua posed the Israelites with a question. Fill in the blanks from Joshua 18:3: How long will you _____ going out to _____ _____ of the land that the Lord, the God of your ancestors, gave you?

- **Page 113, #18** Summarize the primary focus of this section of Scripture in a single sentence.

- Were there any other questions from the Comprehend section that you would like to discuss? Were there any that you weren't sure how to answer, that you were confused about, or that made an impact on you?

Interpret (~20 minutes) – Use this time to discuss what the Biblical text means. You may choose any of the questions from the Interpret section, or use the ones below. Remind everyone that they are welcome to share their thoughts even if they were unable to complete the homework questions.

- **Page 114, #1 (a)** Briefly summarize the Lord's activity. **(b)** What characteristics of God did you notice?

- **Page 114, #3** This week, we were told that the land had been subdued (brought under control) by the Israelites. **(a)** Although the land was subdued, the people were delaying to take possession of it. Why might this have been? List anything that comes to mind. **(b)** What warning does this provide to believers?

- **Page 115, #4** Joshua was unwavering as he exhorted the people to take possession of the land. Turn to pg. 163. What evidence did you see of Joshua's relationship with God in this week's passage? How was Joshua obedient to God? How did Joshua encourage the faith of the people?

- **Page 116, #7** Everyone received an inheritance. However, they did not all receive their inheritance in the same way. **(a)** From the table, how did the Reubenites, Gadites, and the half tribe of Manasseh receive their inheritance? Caleb? Judah, Ephraim, Manasseh West, Benjamin, Simeon, Zebulun, Issachar, Asher and Naphtali? Dan? Joshua? **(b)** How does this challenge your view of receiving spiritual things from God?

- **Page 117, #10** This week, we were told that every promise of the Lord was fulfilled for the Israelites, as the Lord gave them rest on every side. **(a)** The rest God provided through Joshua to the Israelites points to a greater rest for God's people. How did you summarize the message to believer from Hebrews 4:1-11? **(b)** How does this encourage you? How does it challenge you?

- Were there any other questions from the Interpret section that you would like to discuss? Were there any that you weren't sure how to answer, that you were confused about, or that made an impact on you?

Apply (~10 minutes) – During this time, allow participants to talk through how the Lord has been speaking to them personally through this week's study. Have everyone turn to Page 118.

1. To what did the Lord draw your attention this week?

2. How can you respond?

WRAP-UP (~5 minutes)

1. Tell group members: We are nearing the end of this study. I encourage you to KEEP GOING, we are so close! Next week, we'll discuss the Week 8 Listen questions from your study guide.

2. Close in prayer

3. Dismiss to Large Group Teaching time. Teachings are available at www.SeekAndFindStudies.com/Joshua.

A Witness Between Us

GATHER / PREPARE – As participants arrive, greet them and ask them to take a few minutes to skim over their answers to the homework questions, marking anything they would like the group to discuss.

PRAY / REFLECT (~5 minutes) – Open in prayer. Provide a brief summary of what we studied last week, and ask the following:

1. From the Reflect section, what made the most significant impact on you from the past week of study?

2. Was there anything from the teaching that stood out to you?

GROUP DISCUSSION – Remember, you will not be able to discuss every question or address every issue. Your goal is to have a productive discussion that covers the topics most needed by those in your group.

Comprehend (~5 minutes) – Use this time to ensure the group has a good grasp of what the text says. You may choose any questions from the Comprehend section, or use the ones listed below:

- **Page 126, #1** Joshua Chapter 22 begins with Joshua summoning the Reubenites, Gadites and half the tribe of Manasseh. **(a)** What had they done? (22:2-3) **(b)** What had they not done? (22:3) **(c)** What could they now do? (22:4)

- **Page 126, #2** Joshua instructed the two and a half tribes to "carefully obey the command and instruction" that Moses had given them. What was that instruction? Use Joshua 22:5 to fill in the blanks: to _____ the Lord your God,_____ in all his ways, keep his _____, be _____ to him, and _____ him with all your _____ and all your _____.

- **Page 126, #4** As the Reubenites, Gadites, and half the tribe of Manasseh returned to their land, what did they build? (22:10)

- **Page 127 #7** From Joshua 22:16, list the words the Israelites used to characterize what the two and a half tribes had done by building the altar.

- **Page 127, #11** From Joshua 22:26-27: **(a)** What did they say the altar was not built for? **(b)** What did they say the altar was built for?

- **Page 127, #15** Summarize the primary focus of this section of Scripture in a single sentence.

- Were there any other questions from the Comprehend section that you would like to discuss? Were there any that you weren't sure how to answer, that you were confused about, or that made an impact on you?

Interpret (~20 minutes) – Use this time to discuss what the Biblical text means. You may choose any of the questions from the Interpret section, or use the ones below. Remind everyone that they are welcome to share their thoughts even if they were unable to complete the homework questions.

- **Page 128, #1 (a)** What attributes of God did you see the Israelites recognize? **(b)** How did the Israelites' understanding of God impact their actions in this week's text?

- **Page 131, #8** The western tribes had a very strong reaction to what they rightly saw as a very serious offense. **(a)** What might have resulted if the western tribes had avoided conflict with the eastern tribes instead of confronting it? List anything you can think of. **(b)** Sometimes strong responses are necessary. Sometimes soft encouragement is the better approach. How can believers discern which approach to use?

- **Page 132, #9** Joshua demonstrated godly leadership as he sent the eastern tribes home. Turn to pg. 163. What evidence did you see of Joshua's relationship with God in this week's passage? How was Joshua obedient to God? How did Joshua encourage the faith of the people?

- **Page 132, #10** This week, God's people boldly confronted their brothers regarding perceived rebellion against God. Their actions stand as a witness to us today. **(a)** What wisdom do you see in how the Israelites confronted the Reubenites, Gadites, and the half tribe of Manasseh? **(b)** What wisdom do you see in the response of the Reubenites, Gadites, and the half tribe of Manasseh? **(c)** What takeaways do you have from this account?

- Were there any other questions from the Interpret section that you would like to discuss? Were there any that you weren't sure how to answer, that you were confused about, or that made an impact on you?

Apply (~10 minutes) – During this time, allow participants to talk through how the Lord has been speaking to them personally through this week's study. Have everyone turn to Page 134.

1. To what did the Lord draw your attention this week?

2. How can you respond?

WRAP-UP (~5 minutes)

1. Tell group members: Next week is the last week of study and we'll be discussing your answers to the Week 9 Listen questions from your study guide.

2. Close in prayer

3. Dismiss to Large Group Teaching time. Teachings are available at www.SeekAndFindStudies.com/Joshua.

Choose for Yourselves Today

GATHER / PREPARE - As participants arrive, greet them and ask them to take a few minutes to skim over their answers to the homework questions, marking anything they would like the group to discuss.

PRAY / REFLECT (~5 minutes) - Open in prayer. Provide a brief summary of what we studied last week, and ask the following:

1. From the Reflect section, what made the most significant impact on you from the past week of study?

2. Was there anything from the teaching that stood out to you?

GROUP DISCUSSION - Remember, you will not be able to discuss every question or address every issue. Your goal is to have a productive discussion that covers the topics most needed by those in your group.

Comprehend (~5 minutes) - Use this time to ensure the group has a good grasp of what the text says. You may choose any questions from the Comprehend section, or use the ones listed below:

- **Page 143, #4** Read Joshua 23:6-11. List below everything Joshua told the people to do and not to do.

- **Page 144, #10** What three things does Joshua tell the people to do as a result of all the Lord had done for them? (24:14)

- **Page 144, #11** What choice did Joshua place before the Israelites? (24:15)

- **Page 145, #18** Summarize the primary focus of this section of Scripture in a single sentence.

- Were there any other questions from the Comprehend section that you would like to discuss? Were there any that you weren't sure how to answer, that you were confused about, or that made an impact on you?

Interpret (~20 minutes) - Use this time to discuss what the Biblical text means. You may choose any of the questions from the Interpret section, or use the ones below. Remind everyone that they are welcome to share their thoughts even if they were unable to complete the homework questions.

- **Page 146, #1 (a)** Briefly summarize the Lord's activity. **(b)** What characteristics of God did you notice?

- **Page 147, #4** How do the following disciplines help believers ensure we are focused on God and His priorities: Remembrance? Time in the word? Prayer? Biblical community? Serving God? Sabbath (Rest)?

- **Page 148, #8** Joshua wholeheartedly served the Lord and His people all the days of his life. Turn to pg. 163. What evidence did you see of Joshua's relationship with God in this week's passage? How was Joshua obedient to God? How did Joshua encourage the faith of the people?

- **Page 149, #9** Throughout Chapters 23-24, Joshua warned of the dangers of idolatry, abandoning loyalty to God by worshiping and serving other gods. **(a)** Idolatry remains a great danger to believers. What idols did you choose? What does it look like to worship and serve them? **(b)** Anything can become an idol if we trust it more than God, or if it becomes our highest priority. How can believers safeguard against turning God-given resources into idols? **(c)** The Israelites were oblivious that they were doing the very thing Joshua was warning about. How should this impact believers?

- **Page 150, #10** The book of Joshua shows God to be faithful to keep His promises and emphasizes the importance of our faithfulness to Him. **(a)** Joshua told God's people who had already chosen Him, to "choose for yourselves today." What similar message did Jesus give in Luke 9:23? **(b)** Practically speaking, what might this daily choice look like in the life of a believer?

- Were there any other questions from the Interpret section that you would like to discuss? Were there any that you weren't sure how to answer, that you were confused about, or that made an impact on you?

Apply (~10 minutes) – During this time, allow participants to talk through how the Lord has been speaking to them personally through this week's study. Have everyone turn to Page 152.

1. To what did the Lord draw your attention this week?

2. How can you respond?

WRAP-UP (~5 minutes)

1. Tell group members: As we finish our study of the book of Joshua, make sure to take some time this week to complete the Study Reflection on p. 157 of the study guide.

2. Close in prayer

3. Dismiss to Large Group Teaching time. Teachings are available at www.SeekAndFindStudies.com/Joshua.

Important Links

Study Homepage:
https://www.seekandfindstudies.com/joshua

Teachings will be posted on the study homepage weekly.

Follow Seek and Find on Vimeo:
https://vimeo.com/seekandfind

Videos of each week's teaching will be available here.

OR

Subscribe to our channel on YouTube: Seek and Find Studies
https://www.youtube.com/channel/UCUYWS72yzztsNJAHbC8DCGA

Videos of each week's teaching will be available here.

Follow Seek and Find on Facebook:
@SeekandFindStudies

Follow Seek and Find on Instagram:
@SeekandFindCollaborative

Made in the USA
Monee, IL
08 November 2023